*I hope that this volume will satisfy the curiosity
of my two sons, Christian and Stéphane.
It is with great pleasure that I dedicate
this book to them and to all children.*

Lionel GENDRON, m.d.

BIRTH
The story of how you came to be

FOREWORD

Most people feel that the story of life is one of the most fascinating adventures there is. Surely this is because it is such an important part of each of us.

To help you understand the beginning of life, I want to make you a part of the story. I want to show you how your life began just as all life begins. Of course I can't do this without speaking about your father and mother, too. I am also going to invite you to watch the birth of a baby attended by the physician and the nurse.

I think that this explanation of life—of the human egg, of its beginning, of its development, of birth, will help you to attain a healthy attitude towards sexuality.

LIONEL GENDRON, m.d.

BIRTH
The story
of how
you came
to be

LIONEL GENDRON m.d.

Translated by Alice Cowan

**Family Planning Educator — Montreal General Hospital
Secretary, Family Planning Federation of Canada, 1966-1969**

GROSSET & DUNLAP, INC.
A NATIONAL GENERAL COMPANY
NEW YORK, N. Y.

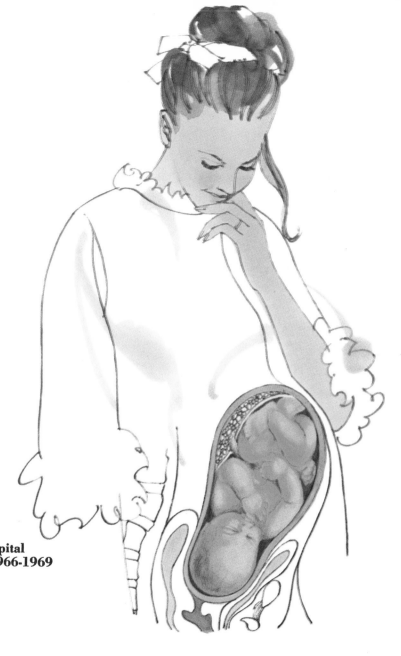

First published in the United States

1972

by **Grosset** & **Dunlap, Inc.**

by arrangement with Harvest House Ltd.

Table of contents

INTRODUCTION

You are a little girl . . . a little boy . . . For some time now you have noticed funny things happening at home. Sometimes in the mornings your mother has been sick to her stomach with what she calls "morning sickness."

During the day, she is more tired than usual. She doesn't play games with you any more, though just a little while ago she liked to do lots of things with you. Now she always seems to be looking for an excuse so that she won't have to take part in what you're doing.

One day you find out why. You had heard your mother complain . . . that she had problems with her waist-line . . . problems about getting too fat, and then you had noticed she had begun to bulge in a really strange way. Some days later your father and your mother told you that soon you were going to have a little brother or a little sister.

And then you had some questions, "Why does having a baby make mother so tired?" . . . "How is the baby made?" "How does it grow?" "How does it come out?"

Of course your parents have tried to explain but you've found some things very difficult to understand. They were even embarrassed, not knowing exactly how to answer your questions. All this made you wonder: "Is it as complicated as that?" Well, yes, it is complicated; but it's simple, too. This is probably why your father and your mother have found it somewhat difficult to answer all your questions.

One day a book was given you which explained these things and which could help you to understand the mysteries of life. It's the book you're looking at now!

You will notice the pictures as you turn the pages, and may feel like going right through the book to look at all the pictures at once; but try not to because you are likely to get confused. Instead read the words that go with each picture; ask your mother or your father to explain what you don't grasp fully in the story or in the pictures. Then you will understand why only women are able to bring children into the world; you will learn how their bodies are made to perform this great and wonderful job.

Before beginning to tell you about the development of a baby, we are going to show you where the baby starts growing in the body of the mother in the first place.

Chapter One

THE REPRODUCTIVE AND SEXUAL ORGANS

First of all, what are reproductive organs?

You've probably already heard of them though you may not have understood much about them. You do know that to breathe, you have lungs. Lungs are called respiratory organs. To digest the food you eat, you have a stomach and intestines which are digestive organs.

Just as we all have lungs so that we can breathe, and a stomach and intestines so that we can digest our food, we all have reproductive organs so that we can have babies when we grow up.

But these organs are different for men and for women. No doubt you noticed a long time ago that boys and girls are not made in the same way.

The reproductive and sexual organs of a man

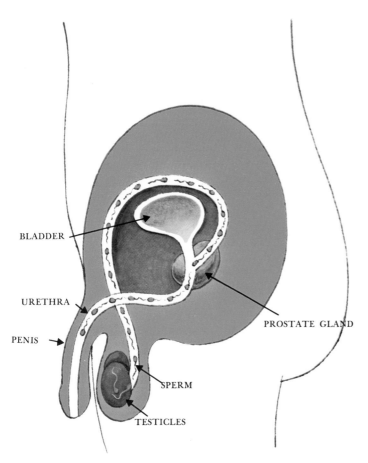

BLADDER

URETHRA

PENIS

SPERM

TESTICLES

PROSTATE GLAND

There are two major organs.
The testicles are like two little balls hung outside the man's body in the crotch between his legs. They are held within a sack of skin called the scrotum.

The penis is an organ which is shaped like a tube. It is just in front of the testicles.

The testicles make sperm; sperm are the reproductive cells of the man. The testicles start making sperm when a boy is around the age of 13 to 15. Each sperm looks like a little tadpole with a roundish head and a long tail which is used to move it along with swimming-like motions. Sperm are extremely tiny and to see them you would need to look through a powerful microscope.

After they have been made, sperm leave the testicles and travel along a little canal called the sperm canal. This takes them right past the prostate gland which is located just beneath the bladder. The prostate makes a special liquid in which the sperm can swim more easily. This liquid with sperm swimming in it is called semen.

Helped along by semen, the sperm continue their journey along another canal called the urethra. The urethra goes right to the end of the penis. If you look carefully at the picture of the reproductive organs of a man, you will notice that the urethra is used both as a way to empty the urine found in the bladder (located above the prostate gland) and as a canal through which sperm may travel. However, this never happens at the same time.

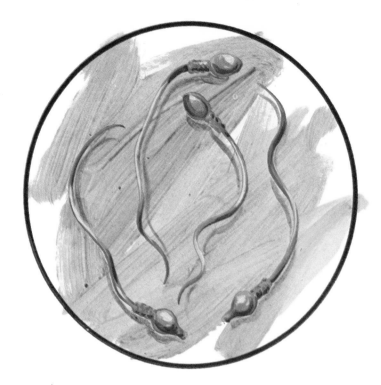

Here is about what you would see if you looked at some sperm cells under a microscope.

The reproductive and sexual organs of a woman

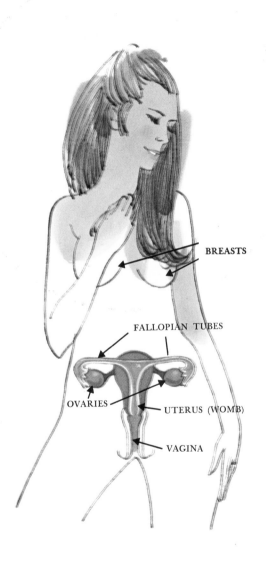

BREASTS

FALLOPIAN TUBES

OVARIES

UTERUS (WOMB)

VAGINA

These organs are:

The vagina

The uterus (or womb)

The Fallopian tubes (two)

The ovaries (two)

The breasts (two)

The vagina is a narrow passage which joins the uterus to the outside of a woman's body. The outside opening of the vagina is in the crotch between the legs. It is protected on the outside by folds of skin called the vulva.

These folds of skin also protect the clitoris and the opening of the urethra. The clitoris is a sensitive organ which can give pleasurable feelings; it is located just in front of the opening of the urethra. The urethra empties urine from the bladder; it opens just in front of the vagina.

There is a third outside opening in the crotch between the legs. This is behind the folds of the vulva; it is called the anus. Like the urethra, it has nothing to do with reproduction. The anus is the opening through which the bowel empties solid brownish waste material called the feces.

Inside is the uterus (or womb). It is the organ in which the impreg-nated human egg develops. The impregnated egg grows and gradually becomes a baby during a pregnancy.

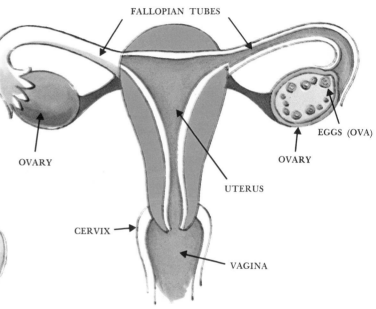

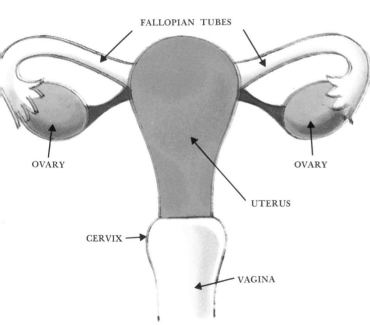

As the baby develops, the womb holding it gets bigger, too.

There is one ovary on each side of the uterus. The two ovaries make the eggs (or ova), which are the reproductive cells of a woman. Though larger than sperm, human eggs are still too small to be seen unless a microscope is used. As you see, the uterus is pear-shaped. Attached to each side of the uterus are two little canals called the Fallopian tubes. These canals connect the uterus to the ovaries.

The breasts are on the outside of the chest of a woman. These organs enable a mother to feed her newly born baby. Milk is made in the breasts, beginning just after the birth of a baby. The mother holds her baby to her breasts so it can suck milk from the nipples.

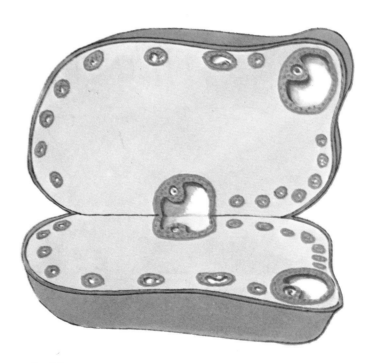

Inside an ovary.

Let's look now at the insides of the uterus (p. 17):

One of the ovaries is shown in cross-section (the right one), so you can see the eggs inside it. And you can see how on each side the Fallopian tubes can guide the eggs towards the uterus. On p. 18 another picture of the in-sides of an ovary is seen. Here, the growing eggs are shown cut in two. To help you understand, this picture is made much larger than an ovary really is. Notice that all along the edge of the ovary are little eggs of various sizes, each enveloped in a little sack. The right and left ovaries

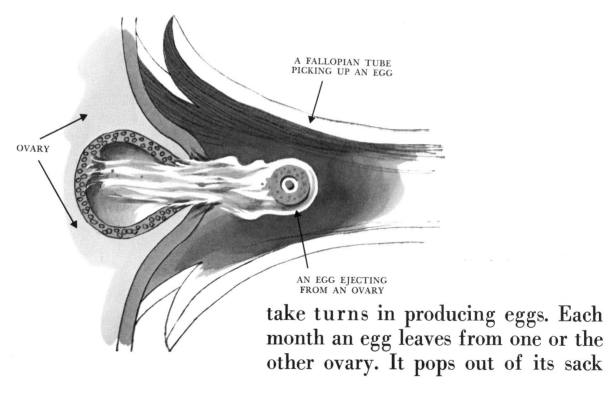

OVARY

A FALLOPIAN TUBE
PICKING UP AN EGG

AN EGG EJECTING
FROM AN OVARY

take turns in producing eggs. Each month an egg leaves from one or the other ovary. It pops out of its sack and out of the ovary and then is picked up by the nearby Fallopian tube.

Now let's look at what happens after the egg is gathered in by the Fallopian tube. The next picture shows you the route that the egg must travel through the Fallopian tube on its way to the uterus.

The egg can't move by itself. But nature has provided other ways to move the egg along the Fallopian tube. These tubes are lined with a furry carpet of hairs which ripple constantly in waves of motion. The egg is moved along almost as though it were on a carpeted conveyor belt.

Each month, the reproductive organs

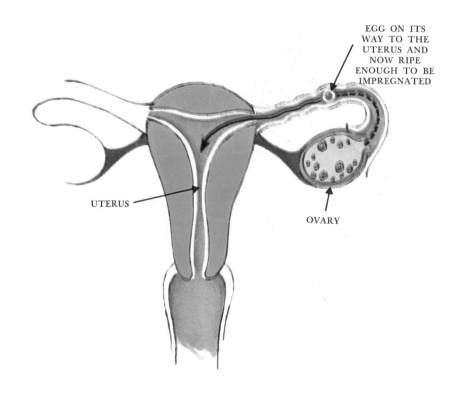

EGG ON ITS WAY TO THE UTERUS AND NOW RIPE ENOUGH TO BE IMPREGNATED

UTERUS

OVARY

change to get ready for a pregnancy. An egg comes along a Fallopian tube and becomes ripe enough to be impregnated by a sperm about half-way along the route between the ovary and the uterus.

The uterus gets ready for a pregnancy by growing a thicker lining. Blood vessels within the lining of the uterus get bigger, making it soft and spongy and ready to nourish a baby.

Usually there is no impregnation, that is usually there are no sperm in the Fallopian tube to meet the ripe egg. The egg is moved on into the uterus and becomes too ripe to be impregnated. Then the extra blood that was stored in the bigger blood vessels along with the extra spongy tissue of the thickened lining is not needed. The extra lining and blood peel off the inside of the uterus and empty outside through the vagina. The egg

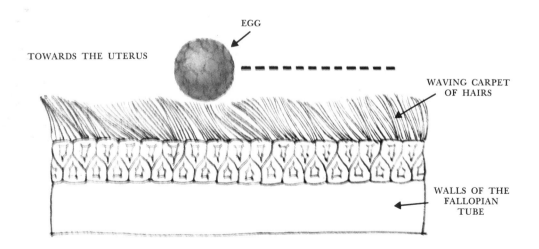

EGG

TOWARDS THE UTERUS

WAVING CARPET OF HAIRS

WALLS OF THE FALLOPIAN TUBE

flows out, too. This is called menstruation or a menstrual period. A period lasts several days and comes at more or less the same time each month.

Usually girls begin to have menstrual periods around the age of 11 or 12 and continue to have them in more or less monthly cycles (unless they are pregnant) until they are 45 to 55 years of age.

You can see by looking at the following pictures what happens every month when there is no pregnancy inside the uterus of girls and women.

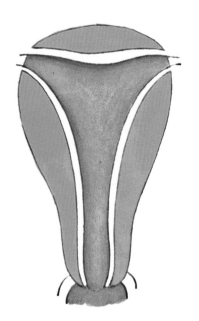

Resting uterus

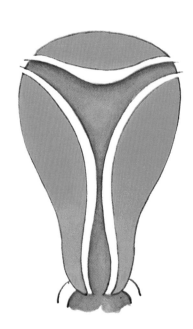

Uterus getting ready for pregnancy. The lining has become much thicker.

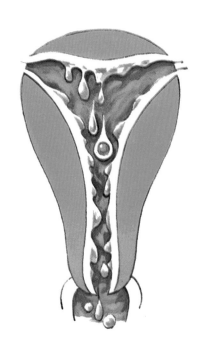

Menstruation starting. The extra blood and the extra lining are emptied out through the vagina.

AT THE BEGINNING OF A PREGNANCY

By now you are probably wondering when a baby is going to come into this story. When I told you that it came from an egg developing inside the body of a woman, you may have thought, "But it's only birds that have eggs!" And yet for humans as well as for all the animals that you see around you, life always starts in an egg. This egg doesn't necessarily look the same as the eggs that you're used to seeing, but the idea is nearly the same and that's what is important. For every kind of animal there is a different kind of egg. There are chicken eggs (these are the ones you know best, of course), frog eggs, sea gull eggs, perch eggs, salmon eggs, and goodness knows how many other kinds.

You may have seen a baby chick come out of its shell sometime when you visited a farm. Or maybe, if you visited the Agricultural Pavilion at the Man and His World Exposition, you will remember having seen the incubator in which you could watch the birth of baby chicks.

What happened inside each of those eggs? When the baby chicken was ready to come out, the chick made pecking movements over and over again inside the egg. It tried gradually to break the shell. And that's what happened as you saw the little chicks born before your eyes. They may have seemed a little wet and forlorn at first, but after a few minutes, they fluffed out and eagerly began their new life on the outside.

But of course the birth of a chick and that of a baby are very different things. Actually, the baby chick develops in an egg outside the body of its mother while the human baby, or the baby cat, or the baby rabbit grows in an egg WITHOUT A SHELL, and it grows INSIDE the body of its mother.

Simply, what is important for you to remember, is that although different kinds of animals are born in different ways, they all begin from an egg, AND SO DO HUMAN BABIES.

Chapter Two

IMPREGNATION

A man and a woman who are married can express their love in many ways.

They are nice to each other, trying to give pleasure to each other, sharing all that they have, sharing sorrows as well as joys.

Often they show their love for each other by cuddling and hugging and saying tender things to each other.

When he does this, a man may show his love for his wife in a very special way: his penis, which is made of spongy tissue, becomes hard. This is a little like when the muscles in the arms of a man rowing a boat become hard, or like the calves in the legs of a bicycle racer when he is making an intense effort.

At the moment when the husband and the wife feel their love become particularly strong, the man is able to push his hard penis into the vagina of his wife. After a few moments semen with many sperm swimming in it spurts out of the husband's penis into his wife's vagina. At this moment the man and his wife may feel a grand physical and mental satisfaction.

The sperm swim from the vagina into the uterus then on up into the Fallopian tubes.

It is in one of the Fallopian tubes that the sperm might meet an egg coming from the ovary. And if you remember, it is in one of these tubes that an impregnation can happen.

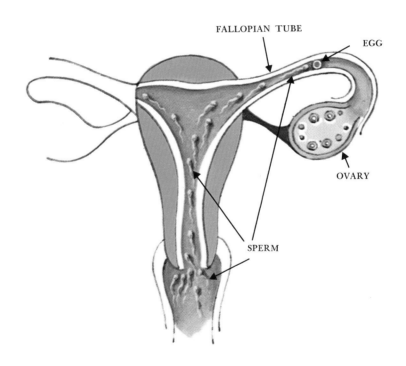

FALLOPIAN TUBE

EGG

OVARY

SPERM

In the preceding picture you can see the sperm which are going to meet an egg that is moving along a Fallopian tube. Sperm are really much tinier than it seems by looking at the picture; they have been greatly enlarged here to help you understand better. Millions of sperm at a time are left in the vagina; thousands enter the uterus; hundreds get as far as the Fallopian tubes. But only a single sperm can impregnate an egg.

Depending on the kind of animal, the number of eggs that can be impregnated at one time varies enormously. In general, only one egg at a time is impregnated in a woman. This number can go up to six for cats and up to 12 for dogs.

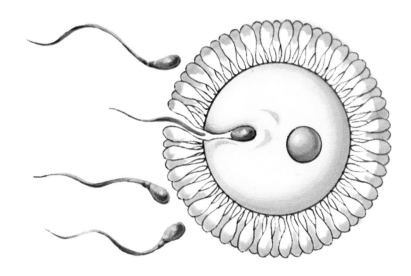

You can see here that only one sperm can push into an egg. Notice that this "privileged" sperm goes directly towards the nucleus of the egg.

Chapter Three

A HUMAN EGG – A BABY

Let's look once again at the preceding picture. We said that only one specially privileged sperm can push into the ovum. What happens then? Its "tail" remains outside the ovum and only its nucleus (its "head") goes to meet the nucleus (or central part) of the ovum. Then these two nuclei, one from the sperm and one from the ovum blend together to form a single cell. It is at this moment that the baby is begun.

The egg has been impregnated; a new life has begun; another human being is about to be created. And this impregnated egg ... it was like you at the beginning of your existence. It was like you before your birth at the time your father and your mother decided to have a child.

Look closely at the following pictures.

In the next two pictures you can see the phenomenon called cell division.

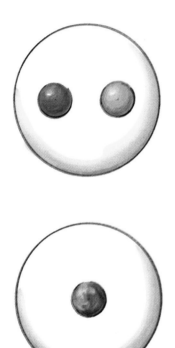

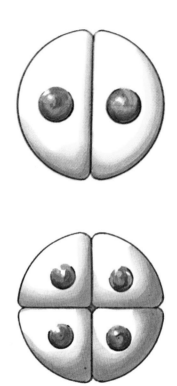

At first, the nucleus of the sperm and that of the egg meet. Then they blend to form a single cell.

The single cell divides. Each new cell contains a replica of the nucleus of the original cell.

Again, the two cells divide to make four cells, each cell carrying its own nucleus identical to that of the original cell.

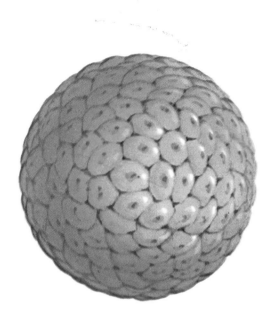

In this last picture, the impregnated egg now has changed so that it looks almost like a raspberry. Each little section represents a cell and by now it would be difficult to count them.

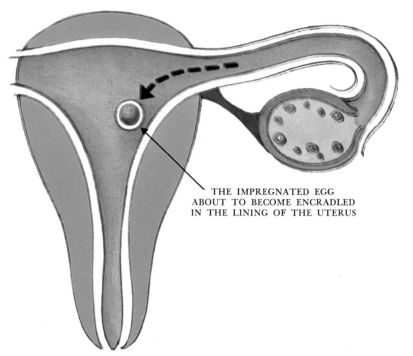

THE IMPREGNATED EGG
ABOUT TO BECOME ENCRADLED
IN THE LINING OF THE UTERUS

Of course all this doesn't happen in five minutes. It took nearly 266 days (or about nine months) from the day of impregnation until the day when you were born.

And this is how you, little boy, or you, little girl who read this book, began. This is how your brother and your sister, your friends and all human beings began. This is how animals, too, began although they do show some differences.

The cells begin to multiply and the impregnated egg is moved along into the uterus where it burrows in to make a cradle for itself.

You saw how each month the lining of the uterus gets ready for a pregnancy. When the ovum is impregnated, the blood vessels in the thickened lining expand so that more blood can come to nourish the new potential human being.

Soon after the new being has become encradled within the uterus it is called an embryo. It will be called an embryo for the first seven weeks of its life. You were an embryo like this once.

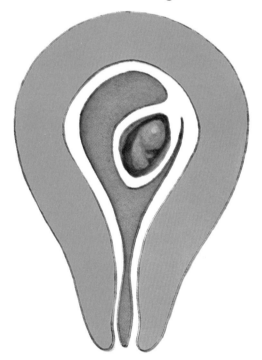

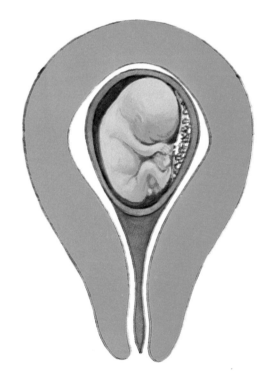

In the picture, the little thing that you see inside the uterus is an embryo. As you can see, it is far from looking like a human.

But here, by eight weeks, you can see that the embryo has the shape of a baby. From this stage until birth, the potential human being is called a fetus.

Let's find out how the cell cluster changes into an embryo.

The first layer of cells in the original ball-like cluster of cells would form your brain, your spinal cord, your nerves, and your skin.

The second layer would make your digestive tract, your liver, your pancreas, and all the organs which allow you to digest your food.

The third layer of cells would turn into your skeleton, your heart, your blood vessels, and your muscles.

But this doesn't happen all by itself. There is a predetermined code, a master plan, in each reproductive cell. Later we'll talk more about this plan that directed the formation of your internal and external organs. However, what it means is that there are never two identical human beings, because there are never two sperms nor two eggs which are exactly identical.

It is because of the master plan that you developed as a human being and not as a fish nor a bird nor a monkey. Human beings of opposite sexes always create humans. In the same way a cow and a bull always have a calf. And in the same way different species cannot mate and reproduce. A dog and a cat, for example, cannot mate to create a young one.

Let's look again at a picture of the first days of your life.

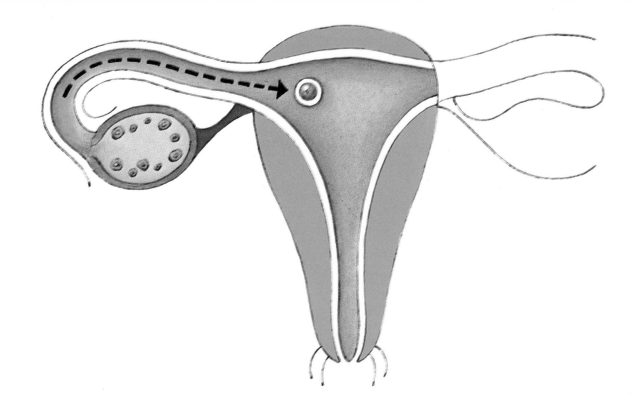

We've already shown the impregnated egg moving towards the uterus along the length of the right Fallopian tube. In this picture we made the egg come along the left tube to show you that the process can occur on either side of the uterus.

It took about one week for the impregnated egg that was you to reach the uterus and to encradle itself in the lining. How about a little arithmetic? If you were going to live about 266 days inside of your mother's abdomen, how many more had you to go by now?

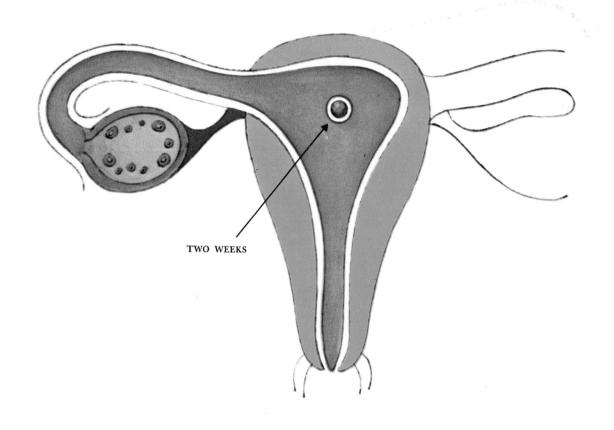

TWO WEEKS

By the end of two weeks, you were just a tiny cluster of cells; however, all the major parts of your body had begun to take shape.

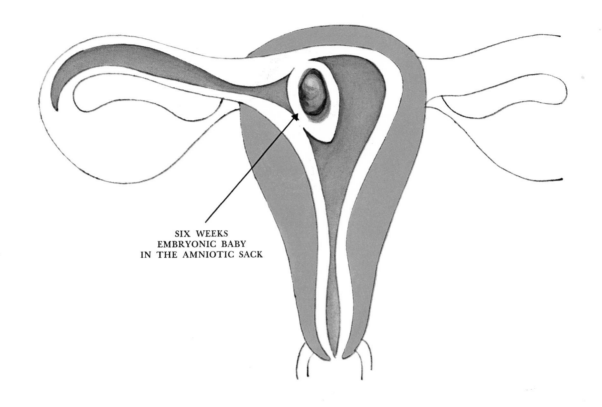

SIX WEEKS
EMBRYONIC BABY
IN THE AMNIOTIC SACK

By the end of six weeks, you were still very tiny but now about one half inch long. If someone could have looked at you, they would have seen that you were surrounded by a transparent sack, a little like a plastic bag.

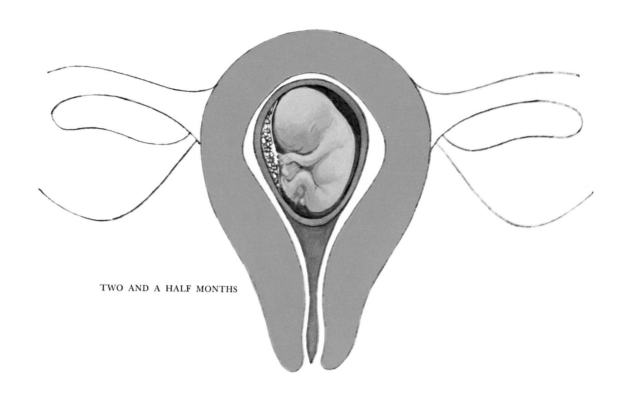

TWO AND A HALF MONTHS

It is called the amniotic sack. It is
filled with a clear liquid which looks
like water and is called amniotic fluid.

You floated inside this fluid almost
like a fish. It acted as a shock

absorber and protected you from knocks and bumps that your mother felt. You were very soft and fragile and needed this protection.

Even at this early time in your life, the outline of your head could have been distinguished as well as your eyes, your ears, your mouth, and your brain. Your heart had already begun to beat.

After about seven weeks, you had grown and become what the doctor called a fetus. You would be called a fetus or a fetal baby until you were born.

By the end of two and a half months, you had begun to look a little more like a baby, but your head was still very large in proportion to the rest of your body. Your eyes would have been clearly distinguishable as well

as your nose and your little arms and legs. Your heart was beating and your kidneys, liver, and stomach were all beginning to take shape.

You would have looked truly human but you were still an extremely tiny being. You measured only an inch in length.

Notice the placenta and the umbilical cord. Their function was to feed you in a completely different way during your fetal stay inside your mother. The placenta is made of many blood vessels, some coming from the fetal baby and some coming from the uterus of its mother. The placenta allows an exchange of food and waste products between the blood system of the mother and the blood system of the fetus. To grow, the fetus needs the nourishment of food, water, and oxygen. All of these necessities come to it from its mother through the intermediary of the placenta and then the umbilical cord.

The umbilical cord is a long tube of tissue which joins the placenta to the fetus through an opening in the fetal abdomen which at birth will permanently close to become the baby's navel.

While you were a fetus, your food came to you from your mother through the umbilical cord. In the same way, you returned your waste products to your mother through the umbilical cord, into the placenta, and then into her bloodstream so that she could eliminate them for you.

By three and a half months inside the uterus, your lips and the muscles of

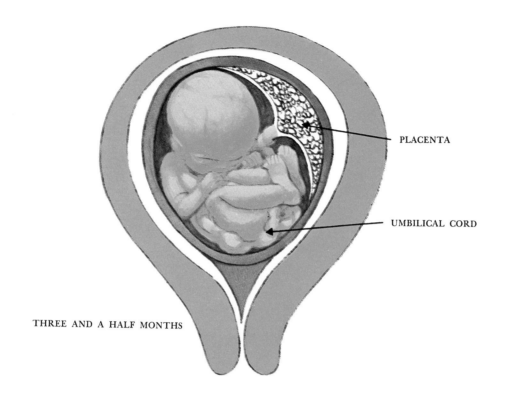

PLACENTA

UMBILICAL CORD

THREE AND A HALF MONTHS

your cheeks had been formed. You now had salivary glands. Slowly you were getting ready to be able to eat and drink by yourself even though you wouldn't be able to use these vital abilities until after you were born.

But this has all been about you. What about your mother? What had been happening to her all this time?

Certainly she had been thinking
about you.

She counted the days because obviously she wanted to hurry up and see you. A baby is quite an event in the life of a family. She had gladly put up with her physical sicknesses.

She probably had had nausea; maybe she had heartburn and stomach ache.

She rested often because she wished the time would pass more quickly until you arrived, but also because she had been more tired than usual.

After all, she always had to carry a little baby around with her.

But you weren't the only thing she had to carry in her abdomen. There were the placenta and the amniotic sack with the amniotic fluid in which you floated. All of this takes up space.

She had to take more care than usual when she moved around especially when going up and down stairs. She didn't want to fall or have an accident. Even though nature had you very well protected in the amniotic fluid, it wouldn't have been very good for you if she had fallen.

Your mother didn't want to have a miscarriage. A miscarriage happens when the little baby fetus comes out into the world much too soon. If it does come out before it is strong enough and before it is sufficiently formed to live outside the body of its mother, it will die.

So you can understand why your mother took such good care of her health.

Your father helped, too. He saw that your mother got enough exercise and fresh air; perhaps he took her walking in the country. And then your parents took quiet moments like these to talk about you.

Yes, it was a big change in their lives...

Now your mother had to take particular care to get the proper nourishment because her diet was yours, too. You had your portion of all that she ate and all that she drank.

She had to be sure to eat a well balanced diet containing a variety of nourishing foods, including fruits, eggs, cereals, milk, and vegetables. There were also vitamins and mineral pills to take to help you have solid bones and shining hair and beautiful fingernails when you were born.

This diet was necessary for her but still more for you. So when she went to the supermarket, she chose her food order with thoughts of the little being that she always carried with her.

She went regularly to the dentist because sometimes mothers develop cavities in their teeth even though they do add extra calcium to their diet by drinking milk and by taking pills. A baby needs lots of calcium and uses most of the extra calcium of its mother.

Each month your mother went to see

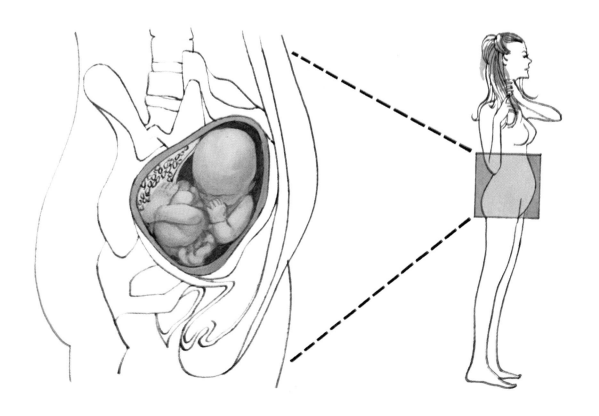

At four and a half months, the fetus takes up practically
all of the extra space within the abdomen of the mother
so her abdominal skin has begun to stretch and bulge
around it. She begins to feel it move.

her doctor to make sure that her pregnancy was normal and that no complication had arisen. The doctor told her to watch her weight to make sure that she didn't gain unnecessarily. It was better for her and for you if she maintained the proper weight.

In short, all that she did, she did with thoughts of you.

During this time you were steadily developing. Some time during the fourth month, you moved. And then, how excited your mother was.

By the time you had been inside your mother for four and a half months, you had begun to be quite active.

You don't remember it, of course, but you turned all sorts of somersaults, all quite automatically. In a way, you moved rather like a fish in the amniotic fluid. However, there wasn't much space.

Your mother was very conscious of your movements. You would give her kicks with your foot, jabs with your elbow, and even punches with your fist when you wanted to move.

Sometimes, you had hiccups. Like a real baby you had hours when you slept and hours when you were awake. You probably sucked your thumb.

By six months, you had become even more interesting. You measured 13 to 14 inches in length and you weighed a little more than a pound. This didn't make you very big, perhaps, but you gained strength day by day.

Your eyelids opened. You could look up, down, and around. Of course you couldn't see anything. One reason could have been because you found yourself in the dark, but really it was because even a little baby that has just been born can see nothing during the first four or five days (after that, it begins to distinguish shadows or the difference between light and dark).

Your mother began to feel light, quick contractions of the uterus after you had been inside her for about seven and a half months. She often thought that you were ready to make

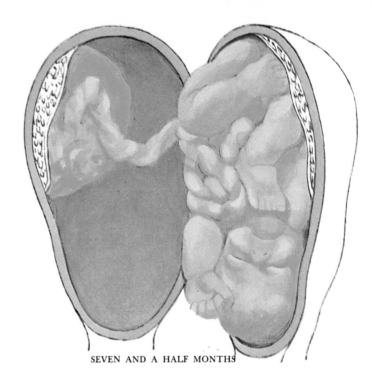

SEVEN AND A HALF MONTHS

The fetus at seven and a half months. If the baby were born at this time, it could survive in an incubator.

This was a premature baby, that is a baby born before it had lived nine months inside the uterus. It must spend several weeks in an incubator, like this one, where it can receive oxygen and food so that it can grow strong enough to live a normal life outside of the machine.

48

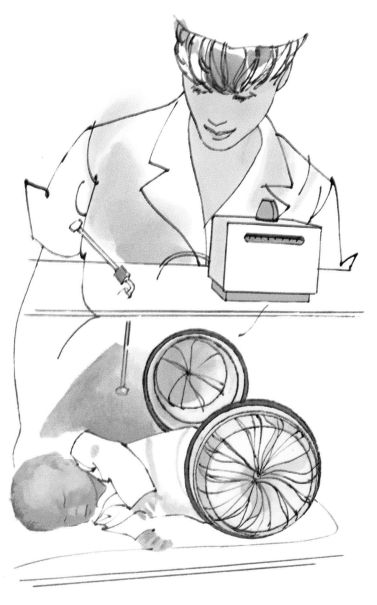

your appearance into the world. She had to rest more than usual because the load she held was becoming more and more cumbersome and more and more difficult to carry. Your weight with the amniotic fluid, the placenta, and the enlarged uterus–all this was very heavy to hold.

But the uterus grew calm again and you continued your intra-uterine life (that is your life inside the uterus). You may be wondering about now, "If I had been born at that moment, if I had left the abdomen of my mother, would I have lived?"

In answer, about all we can say is that with good care and a stay of several weeks in a machine called an incubator, your chances of survival would have been very good.

An incubator is like a glass cage which is heated inside to the same temperature as inside a mother's abdomen. It is similar in a way to the incubators used by poultry breeders to hatch baby chicks.

The eighth month arrived. Your mother began to get worried because she couldn't feel you move any more.

She could no longer feel the little blows from your foot, your fist, or your elbow.

So she went to see her doctor. And he, with the help of an instrument called a stethoscope, was able to hear the beating of your heart. This stethoscope is like a tiny microphone attached to the ears of the doctor by rubber or plastic tubes. By placing the stethoscope on the abdomen of your mother and listening carefully, he was able to hear your heart beating.

He soon made clear the mystery of your inactivity. You were probably turning fewer somersaults because you had grown and the space inside your mother's abdomen was now so tight. You just didn't have any room to move.

Your mother returned from the doctor reassured, knowing that you were alive and well inside her.

Finally the ninth month arrived and your mother's problems became more acute because you now weighed six pounds! Without a doubt, you had

really become a lovely baby, ready to be born. You already had lots of hair and well formed fingernails. In fact your fingernails were so long that they would have to be cut right after your birth. Usually it is necessary to cut the fingernails of a baby several days after its birth because otherwise, as it makes uncoordinated movements with its hands, it scratches its face.

Slowly but surely, you were getting ready to come out into the world. You now found yourself upside down. By the ninth month, you pointed your head towards the vaginal canal of your mother. Your head was just over the way out located between her legs.

Usually when babies are ready to be born, they turn head downwards automatically. The head is the heaviest part of a baby. (Have you ever looked at a new baby and noticed that its head is very large in proportion to the rest of its body?) This head downwards position is probably the one in which the fetus is most comfortable and probably that's why it turns into this position.

At the last appointment with the doctor before your birth, the doctor told your mother that you were in a good position and that you were all ready to be born.

Sometimes it isn't so simple because the baby presents its seat first, that is, it points its bottom rather than its

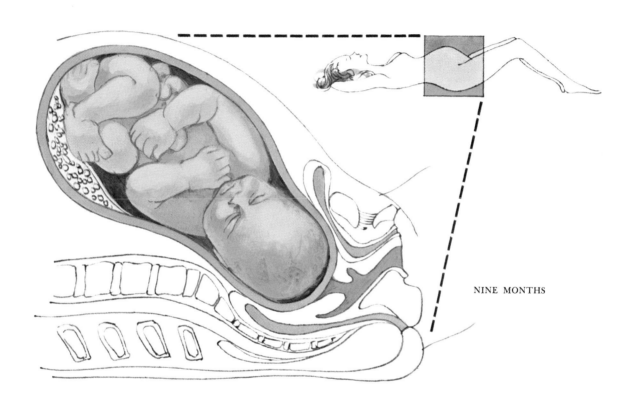

NINE MONTHS

This picture shows the baby in head first position ready
to leave the uterus.

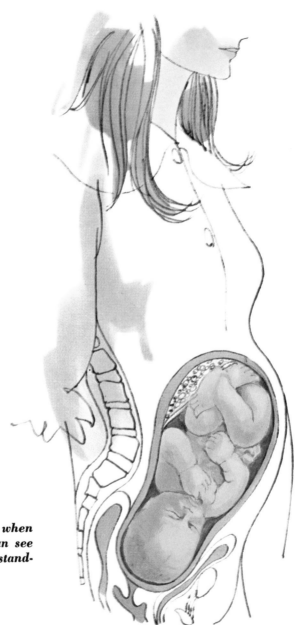

In the last picture you saw how the baby is placed when the mother is lying down. In this picture you can see how the baby is upside down when the mother is standing, at the ninth month of a pregnancy.

head towards the vaginal exit. In these cases, the birth is normal but it is much more difficult for the mother.

In short, at the end of the ninth month, you were ready to be born; your nerves and your muscles were working together to organise your arrival into the outside world.

By this time you were big and strong. You weighed about seven pounds. You were ready to swallow and to digest the food of a new-born. You could almost see; you were able to hear, breathe, feel hot and cold—all like a real baby. You were really too big to live inside the uterus of your mother. It was time to leave and to show yourself to your parents who were terribly impatient to meet you.

But, alas, babies don't know how to read calendars! Your mother counted the days and the hours. Your father did, too. But they could only wait and try to be patient...

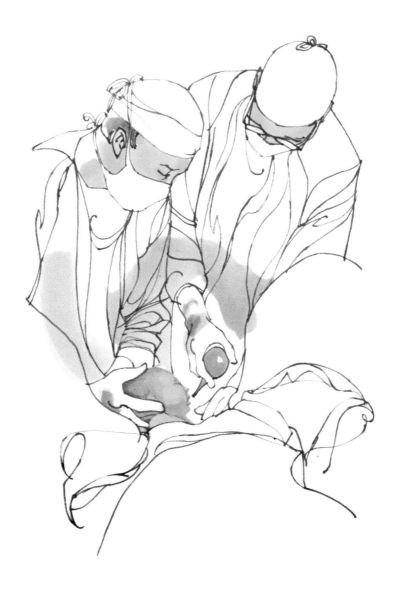

Chapter Four

THE BIRTH

Finally, it was your big day!

Your mother began to feel contractions of the muscles of her uterus. This is called labor. At the beginning the contractions weren't very frequent. Several hours before your birth, she began to feel them every five minutes and then your father took her to the hospital. If you were her first baby, the labor probably lasted about 15 hours. That would be usual.

After she had been in the hospital a while, your mother felt some good hard contractions and your head appeared. The doctor helped to free your head and then your shoulders. The rest of your body followed easily.

And there you were finally in the outside world!

The doctor held your head; and his assistant, with a little rubber syringe, cleared out the mucus found in your nose, mouth, and throat, so that you could breathe. And then you cried and showed the world that you were living. Your lungs had been filled with air for the first time.

Now let's see step by step how your birth proceded.

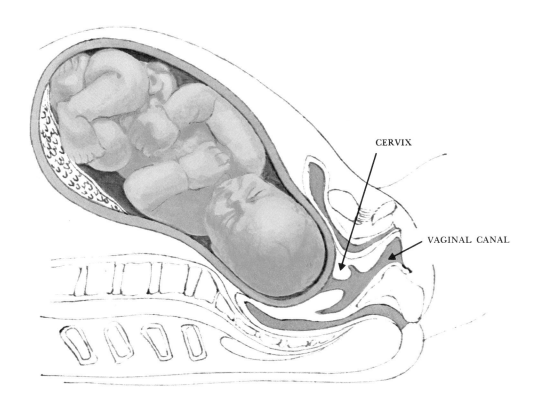

CERVIX

VAGINAL CANAL

In the picture you can see the baby just before its birth. Notice the cervix which is the bottom part of the uterus surrounding the opening to the vagina. The vagina is also called the birth canal since it is the passage through which the baby must pass during its birth.

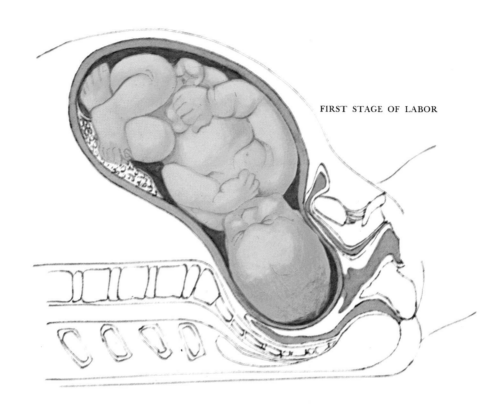

FIRST STAGE OF LABOR

This is the first stage of labor. The contractions of the uterus are slowly causing the cervix to open to allow the baby's head through.

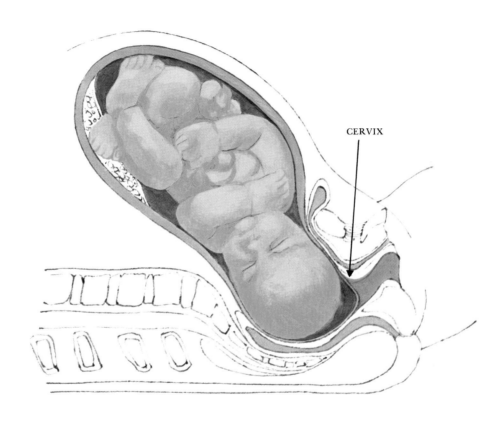

CERVIX

*The baby descends little by little. The cervix becomes
thinner and thinner until it is almost as thin as a sheet
of paper.*

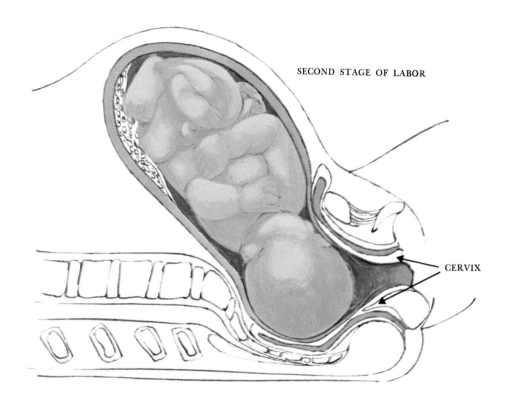

SECOND STAGE OF LABOR

CERVIX

This is the second stage of labor. The cervix is completely open. The mother, along with the contractions of her uterus, can now use her abdominal muscles to help push the baby into the vaginal canal.

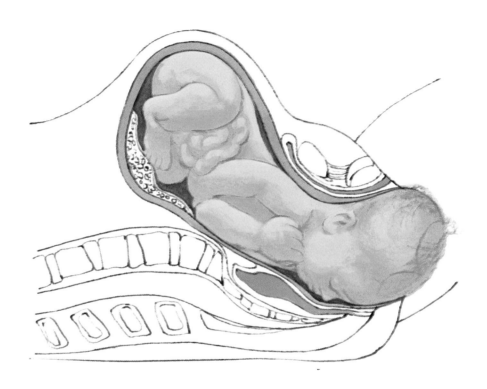

The crown of the head is beginning to show outside. Notice how it is slightly misshapen and how it pivots to one side so that it adapts itself to the shape of the vaginal canal. The bones of a baby's skull are separated by soft margins called fontanels. These enable the head to become moulded into a shape that allows an easier birth. If you have ever seen a newborn baby, you may have noticed that its head was slightly misshapen. This is natural; the skull will regain its normal shape some time after the birth of the baby.

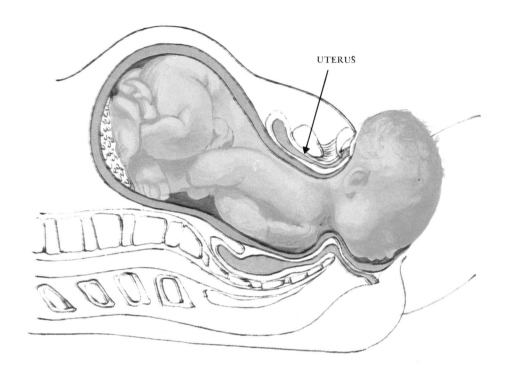

UTERUS

This is almost the time of the baby's birth. The crown of the head can clearly be seen from the outside. Notice how the uterus of the mother is getting smaller and smaller as it empties itself.

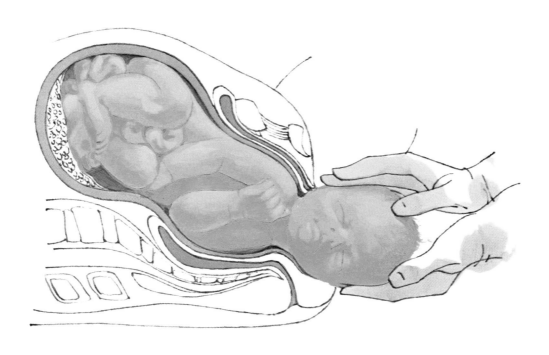

Finally the birth!
The doctor's hands guide the head and the shoulders of
the baby to avoid tearing the tissues of the mother.

This is about what you looked like immediately after your birth. Notice that you still were joined to your mother by the umbilical cord. Just about now you cried for the first time.

Chapter Five

AFTER THE BIRTH

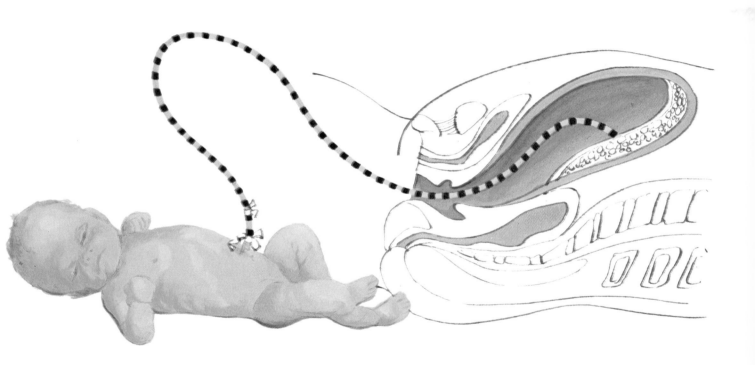

Now you had become a part of the world. The doctor cut your umbilical cord between the two knots he had tied around the cord—almost like you can see in the picture.

The doctor showed you to your mother and then he sent you to the nursery where a nurse washed you, put drops in your eyes, and dressed you.

The nurse then took your footprints so that you could be identified, since newborn babies look much alike. Then she put you in a crib near other newborn babies. Except when you were with your mother, you lived there during the next five or six days and waited until your mother left the hospital.

During this time, what was happening to your mother? For some minutes after your birth, her uterus continued to contract until the umbilical cord and the placenta (now called the afterbirth) had been pushed out. Then your mother's labor was finished. Things had gone well for both you and her. This was a great relief for your mother.

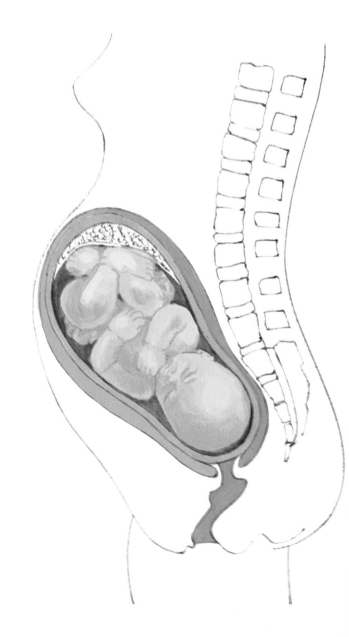

Let's go back a little and look again at the picture showing all the space you had taken up in your mother's abdomen.

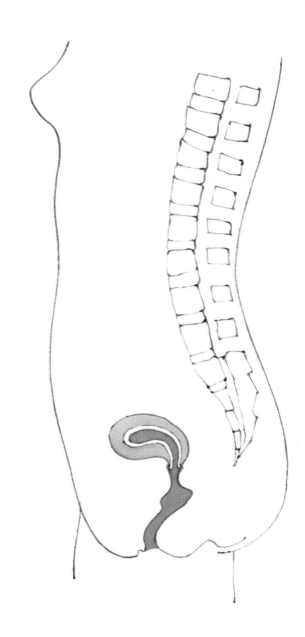

Compare the last picture with this one. This one shows the size of your mother's uterus some weeks after your birth. There certainly is a difference, isn't there?

Immediately after your birth, the doctor went to congratulate your father. He told him that everything had gone normally. Your father couldn't wait to see you.

So the nurse brought you to your father and she congratulated him, too. At last your father could see you and try to find out who you most looked like.

Then it was time for your father to go to congratulate your mother. He told her that she had been wonderful and that she had done a splendid job. Maybe he even told her that the baby was as beautiful as she was!

Very happy, your father went to telephone all the relatives: grandfathers, grandmothers, aunts, uncles, and all of his friends, too. He was just full of praises for his baby. His relatives and friends replied that they, too, couldn't wait to see you.

Twelve hours after your birth, you were hungry and wanted to eat. Your mother gave you her breast. You sucked her milk naturally; you probably learned how by sucking your thumb during your life inside the uterus.

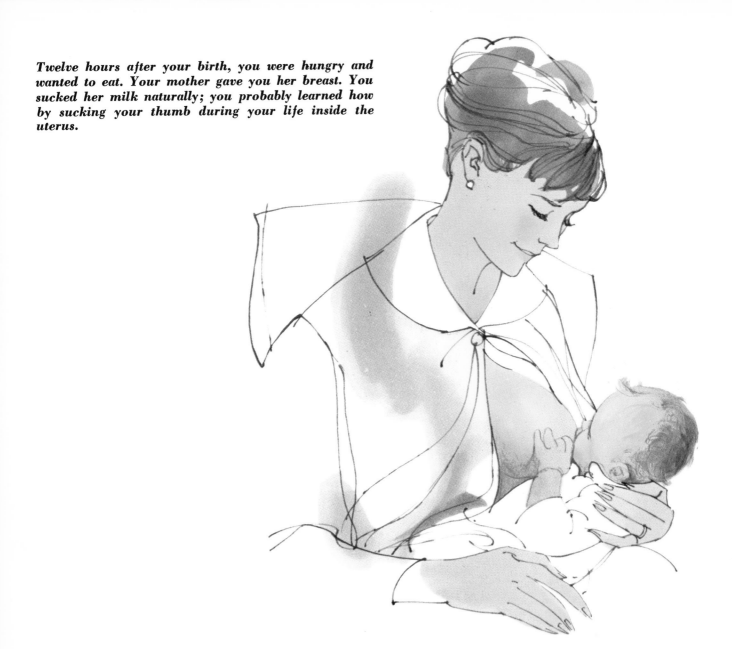

About the fifth day after your birth, you left the hospital with your mother. Friends and relatives waited for you at the house and it was with great joy that they made your acquaintance.

Chapter Six

WHY TWINS?

Sometimes a mother gives birth to more than one child at a time. In fact, in each hundred mothers having a baby, there will be one who will have twins.

Rarer still, that is about one time in 10,000, three babies (or triplets) come into the world at the same birth.

There are also quadruplets and even quintuplets (that is four or five babies coming into the world at the same birth), but these cases are so rare that they are reported immediately in the news media.

We saw that a woman's ovary ordinarily sends just a single egg at a time into the nearby Fallopian tube and that only this egg could be impregnated. Sometimes two eggs are ejected at the same time by an ovary and each of these eggs is impregnated in the Fallopian tubes by a different sperm (look again at the pictures in the first chapter). If this happened, that is if there were two impregnated

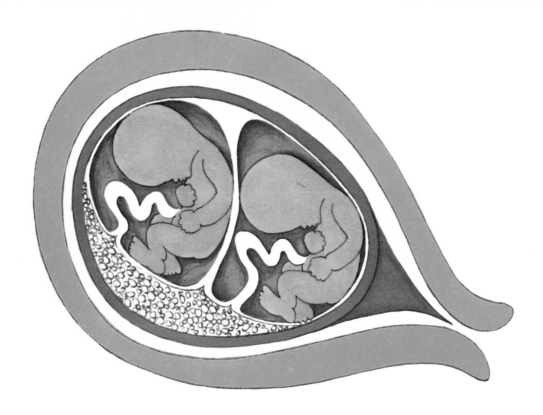

In this sketch, you can see how twins are placed in the
uterus of their mother. These are true twins because
they are nourished from the same placenta. Though all
twins have their own umbilical cords and their own
amniotic sacks, only true twins use the same placenta.
Non-identical fraternal twins have each their own placenta. The twins which you see here are not completely
developed. They will soon get into a position like the
one you can see in the next picture.

eggs, then two distinct babies would grow both at the same time inside the uterus of their mother. When they were born, they probably wouldn't even look like one another. One could be a boy and the other could be a girl.

One could be brunette, and the other could have red or chestnut coloured hair. In fact, the two babies would be as different as children born during the course of two different pregnancies. They would have resemblances in the same way that any two children born of the same parents would have. These kinds of twins are called fraternal twins.

How are "true twins" formed, those twins that look as alike as two peas in a pod? Their formation is very different from that of fraternal twins. It all happens at the beginning of the division of the primary cell created by the impregnated human egg.

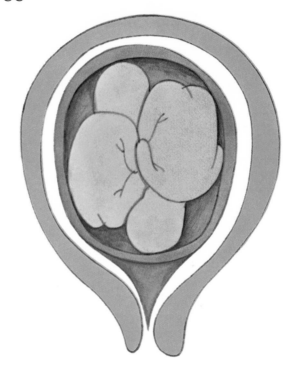

Once the first twin has left the uterus, the second will probably turn itself upside down, or maybe he will present himself bottom first. This depends upon the birth; each case is different.

Notice how the two cells coming from the primary cell separate so that each forms an individual cluster. That is, two human beings will be formed from the same primary cell. These will become true identical twins.

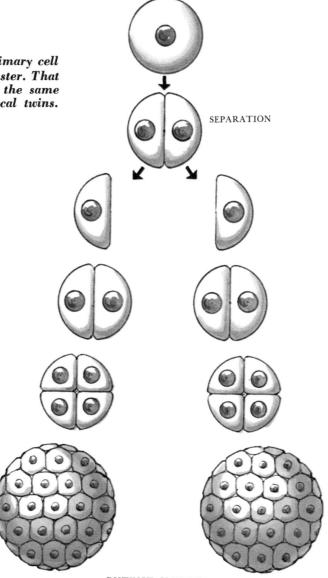

SEPARATION

DISTINCT CLUSTERS

You saw in the third chapter that this primary cell divided first into two and then into four until it formed a cluster of cells which looked like a raspberry. At the moment when it normally would have divided into four, the two cells which had come from the primary cell separated from each other and each began to develop its own cluster of cells which began to grow into separate human beings (look at the pictures on page 30 and then back to those on page 82). As you can see, these separate clusters which will become true, identical twins, began from a single egg impregnated by a single sperm.

In the case of triplets or of quadruplets or of quintuplets, the same rules apply. Maybe three, four, or five eggs were impregnated at the same time or maybe one impregnated egg began to make others and didn't follow the usual rules of cell division. It kept making separate cells, each becoming eventually a distinct embryo and then fetus and then baby.

Chapter Seven

WHY ARE ALL HUMAN BEINGS DIFFERENT?

Why are there men, women, blacks, whites, yellow people, people with blond hair, brown hair, red hair, people with eyes that are blue, hazel, green, or gray?

Why is it that there is no one person who is exactly like his neighbour or his brother or his sister (even with true twins there are little differences that are quite obvious)?

In the third chapter when we spoke about the different layers of cells which formed your brain, your spinal cord, and so on, we said that there is a pre-established code which directs all this and that this code is found in each reproductive cell. This pre-established code, this master plan, is part of the wonder of creation; it is called heredity.

Each reproductive cell, that is each sperm and each egg is different from any other; each possesses its own distinct personality.

We saw how in each egg and in each sperm there is a nucleus. If you looked at this nucleus under a very powerful microscope, you would be able to see things that look like little sticks. These are called chromosomes.

Each paternal reproductive cell, that is, each sperm, contains 23 chromosomes. Each maternal reproductive cell, that is, each egg, contains an equal 23 chromosomes. When the sperm and the egg blend to create a human cell or a primary cell, this founding cell contains 46 chromosomes grouped together in pairs.

Each of the 23 chromosomes from the sperm has found a matching chromosome within the egg, and so there are 23 pairs of chromosomes blended together in the primary cell of the new human being.

Every cell which is formed after the primary cell will also contain these 23 pairs of chromosomes and all the characteristics belonging to them, which have come from the father and the mother.

Special chemical substances called genes are carried on each of these chromosomes. There are very many genes; they look like fine threads.

To give you an idea of the size of these genes, think about a single chromosome (which is itself microscopic).

Each single chromosome can hold nearly a thousand genes. This is hard to imagine, but it's true.

These genes have a very important role to play because it is they which contain the mysterious pre-established code, the master plan with its information and directions. In sum, it is the genes which determine how every new living being will be formed.

These genes come from both the father and the mother, and blend into a unique combination of characteristics which make an individual unlike anyone else that ever lived—even the father or the mother.

People may say to you, "You have blue eyes from your mother. Your nose is from your father. You are quick like him. When you do such and such a thing you are just like your mother..." but you are really just you. Even when you were only a microscopic egg, you were already just yourself; you were a unique individual; you had a personality unlike anybody else that ever

lived—even your father or your mother.

When your father was born, his chromosomes and his genes came from his

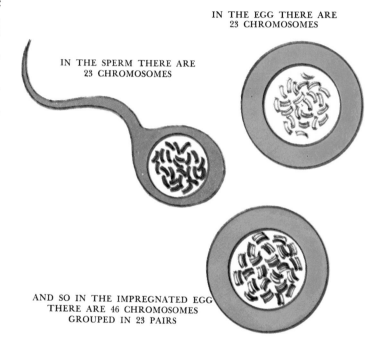

IN THE EGG THERE ARE
23 CHROMOSOMES

IN THE SPERM THERE ARE
23 CHROMOSOMES

AND SO IN THE IMPREGNATED EGG
THERE ARE 46 CHROMOSOMES
GROUPED IN 23 PAIRS

The male and female reproductive cells (sperm and egg) each contain 23 chromosomes. After joining together to form a primary human cell, the two groups of 23 chromosomes match into pairs, making 46 chromosomes altogether. These chromosomes carry thousands of the genes which determine the physical qualities and the personality type of each new human being.

father and from his mother. It was the same for your mother. Her father and her mother transmitted to her some of the chromosomes and some of the genes that they had received in turn before from their parents. And so, on and on back one could go. This is heredity.

You may be a bit sickly. You may seem to catch all the colds that are around. If anyone studied this carefully they might find out that your grandfather or your grandmother was also subject to colds and chills.

Or let's suppose that you are allergic to animal hair or to certain fruits.

We might discover very quickly that your mother reacted in the very same way.

Many things are due to heredity.

Maybe they say at school that your I.Q. is very high. Who is responsible? Perhaps your mother, your father, your grandfather, who knows? Maybe further back than that we could find a particularly brilliant ancestor of yours.

You may have blue eyes, brown skin, or blond hair. Your face may be oval-shaped or square. Your ears may be small like your mother's. The shape of your mouth may be like your father's mother's; the arrangement of your teeth may be like those of your mother's father's; and maybe you have to wear braces because those teeth don't fit with that size mouth! This is still due to the genes randomly transmitted to you by your parents.

Whether we inherit the good or the bad qualities of our parents, it is always by chance. Every sperm or egg carries a different mixture of 23 of the total 46 chromosomes available from each parent. Thus the new human cell is not determined in exactly half of its characteristics by the father and half by the mother.

The element of chance aside, some genes are more dominant than others. For example, the gene regulating the brown colour of eyes is more dominant than that which makes eyes blue. (If a primary cell received one gene from its father calling for brown eyes and one matching gene from its mother calling for blue eyes, the primary cell would produce a baby with brown eyes because the gene for brown eyes is dominant and wins every time!

But that brown-eyed child would carry a blue-eyed gene within its genetic master plan even though it didn't show on the outside. When that child grows up, if it mates with a blue-eyed person, then it could have a blue-eyed baby because half of its reproductive cells would carry the blue-eyed gene from its mother.)

Genetics or the study of heredity is a wonderful and difficult subject that could be discussed for hours!

Will it be a boy or a girl?

Do you wonder why you are a boy rather than a girl... a girl rather than a boy?

Now that you have learned something about heredity, this problem can be solved because the sex of the newborn child is also determined by the set of chromosomes.

Half of the paternal reproductive cells (the sperm) contain a sex chromosome of the type called "X" and the other half have a chromosome of the type called "Y." However, the maternal reproductive cells (the eggs) all contain just one kind of sex chromosome—of the type called "X."

Among the 23 chromosomes from the egg, there is only a single sex chromosome called "X." Among the 23 chromosomes from the sperm, there is only a single sex chromosome which may be either the one called "X" or the one called "Y."

If the sperm that unites with the egg contains a sex chromosome called "X," then the baby will be a girl.

That is:

X + X = GIRL

If the sperm that unites with the egg contains a sex chromosome called "Y," then the baby will be a boy.

That is:

X + Y = BOY

So you can see that it was quite by chance that you turned out to be a girl or boy.

This is why the sex of any new baby is a surprise and this is why parents without taking their preferences into account must accept their newborn child with joy regardless of its sex. And so you have the wonderful story of birth, one of the most extraordinary stories that you could be told.

It is a story that is repeated every day, every hour, and every minute, in every corner of our world.